www.finishinglinepress.com

East Rock

poems by

Paul Stroble

Finishing Line Press
Georgetown, Kentucky

East Rock

For Beth and Emily,

and in memory of Dr. Carol Thysell

Publisher: Leah Huete de Maines
Editor: Christen Kincaid
Cover Art: "East Rock" by John Ferguson Weir (1906)
Author Photo: Jeannie Liautaud Photography, LLC
Cover Design: Elizabeth Maines McCleavy

Order online: www.finishinglinepress.com
also available on amazon.com

Author inquiries and mail orders:
Finishing Line Press
PO Box 1626
Georgetown, Kentucky 40324
USA

Contents

Julia B. Rosenbaum is author of the book, *Visions of Belonging: New England Art and the Making of American Identity* (Ithaca: Cornell University Press, 2006). One of the paintings she discusses is Marsden Hartley, *The Last of New England—The Beginning of New Mexico* (1918/1919). Hartley paints scenes of New England and of the Southwest as if they bordered, separated only by a run-down fence. The painting suggests the American captivation with Western regions (leaving though not abandoning the historic Northeast), and diversity in the sense of place. Hartley also appreciated Native American traditions (Rosenbaum, pp. 153-155, and Plate 4). Her discussion of the painting inspired me to write this poetic conflation of New England and the Southwest, based on my own experiences, family, and interests.

I

Northeastern Eden

New Haven, 2022

Forty years ago
I drove up to an ATM on Whitney Ave.
    for a student's frugal twenty—

accompanying the generous cliff

ninety meters high,
            reddish trapp and fractured scree,
                    the memorial, lonely then,
            for the war dead's honor.

East Rock is part of the Metacomet Ridge,

    Amherst to East Haven,
different lava flows with different formations,

tremors of Pangea
        breaking—
                Africa, Europe, America,
move like Noah's nations.

    God said, let lava cool to tap rock—
what white men named New England—

            lithify, O sediment, to sandstone,
let erosion destroy so layers lift.

God said, let there be chestnut oaks
            and red cedar,
                    let the plants show
that life cannot be canceled,

            let them thicken into wilderness
                    and be filled with eastern birds.

*

The ridge is no geography
        formed into shape

by primordial chaos and Noah's flood,
        what we call the Atlantic sweeping up basalt
from the earth's molten center,

                an easy fit for Moses' scriptures and
Neptunian faith: Earth's layers and
                features formed from
the rising, setting of the waters.

        Those years of faith's shock,
the catastrophic findings of James Hutton,
        Charles Lyell,

        that the earth was always as it is
now, and alters slowly, creating

uniform changes over epochs
        of which Genesis has no record.

        Silliman had difficulty, too,
                Yale's science master,
                        careful to step up
to Plutonian fires
        even as he pointed the way
                for petroleum's worth—

(I stood in the cold
        past Natural History
                at the corner of Silliman College,

of double mind, my New Testament class
        this way but a goof-off trip
to the Co-op that way)—

too Puritan, too literal
        and too analogical alike,

as if the land
rose from the waters English.

*

But there's a story arc
from Genesis 1
across the generations of Abraham and Sarah

to the plain of Rahah and Sinai:
when You blessed the Sabbath,

covenant with Your people everlasting

for love of living things
and *Tikkun Olam*.

Bezalel of Judah, Oholiab of Dan,
and every able man

whose heart was stirred
crafted tent and ark and mercy seat,

altar, lampstand, and laver,
to guide Israel through its long sojourn.

Sinai foreshadowed the shores
of Gilgal, Glory reliable.

Those were wilderness days,
but no matter,
for Sinai
was not home,
to show that every place
is the place of righteousness,

creation is of the Lord,

and each human life
is sacred.

*

If I could paint in Hudson River style
all the landscapes that are our souls

shared by all.
Artists dabbed their antebellum palettes:
the cliffs
and a horseback ride in autumn,

women with baskets, a child,
a rider,
hay standing before
boatmen on the Mill River
and New Haven chimneys

as Eden grows industry.

The flowers, fields, and butterflies.

I'd do nothing else
but render the land as iconography
until I ask once more for mercy
and go down to the dead till Heaven,

while my carved name remains
on oil paintings of tree trunks,
and folks would depart in tears
from the beauty
I rendered,

a well-meaning amateur.

*

The grand, granite pedestal
and tapered shaft is memory art
atop East Rock
for the war dead of New Haven,

years in the works. A lawsuit, assurance

from up in Hartford, money raised
               with confidence,
     quarrels about the design,
and about catered food:

the Angel of Peace knows our frame.

Nearly 200,000 showed up
          and 20,000 marched
with bright flags and banners
          for the 1887 dedication.

     Sherman was there,
and Sheridan, heroes of the war
               and of the West.
     It rained. No matter.
There was satisfaction all around
               for a needful thing,
     each honored human name.

(When you've no relatives
          on a monument,
no name stands out.)

Do I remember right
          that forty years ago, the stones
were tagged, like bright ribbons strewn
          when kids
tear open gifts? Cities struggled
          in those days.

     But the place looks good today.

We saw visitors and hikers and children
          on a sunny afternoon,
a loving view of the valley,

     remembrance of war's hard hand.

*

The ridge remembers another hero,

        Metacomet, "King Philip,"
    Wampanoag sachet
who saw no possibility of peace
        except to be pushed West, harassed,
after the death of his father Massasoit.

        We know him, if at all,
from his vast nomenclature:

    the Metacomet Ridge
northward,
      and his quartz seat in Rhode Island,

Metacomet streets and restaurants,
      apartments and recreation.

Yes, they feel so New England to me.
      so comforting,
    American—

And the thousands of Indian place names
      across the country
    like the very words
Massadchu-es-et, Quinnehtukqut—

    while I sit at my windows
and read books of destiny.

*

    Across the valley,
      love for West Rock, too,
and my memories of classmate trips with buddy Joyce
      to the country book barn.

Look over from the road
      across West River to boulders
    amid the diabase,
remote and secure enough

for Judges Goffe and Whalley
to spend a refugee
        Connecticut summer
while the colonial governor

        held up messengers
with the royal order of arrest,

        no Restoration pardon
for Roundhead signers
        of the king's death warrant.

I think the stones looked better
        in Frederick Church's painting,
as they would—
        his Hudson River truth.

        Lucky Dixwell—John Davids,
he called himself—
        thought dead, rode down
to New Haven to join them,

        regicides aiming someday to blend in.
Cruel necessity, muttered Cromwell

        at the royal casket, as now we teach
the decades bleak with religion, martyrs

        the seed of both congregations.

(1676, and as King Philip's War raged
        out of modern Anglo mind,

        to burn one side and the other
and drive the English into the sea,

they say that Goffe himself—missing for years—
        appeared, grave and odd

during an attack and led
        the colonists to victory

as if a bridge to American identity
from the blood of England

then he disappeared, like
an angel sent of God, said Ezra Stiles.)

One day, we walked down to the Green
with friends' well-worn inside jokes

as Englishmen in flight
shared light words to pass
uncertain days;
central church in sight

of dear Old Campus,
John Dixwell's grave:

buried in secret in a new land,
no heads now
for London Bridge.

*

Legend was that Ezra Stiles—
respected president
wrangling pious students
clamoring for better food—

adopted for Yale's shield
the name of the objects on the breastplate
of the High Priest,

Urim v'Tummin,
lux et veritas, Light and truth,

verity and illumination
on our beloved shields
for education, scholarship,
once solely for the training of clergy.

What a blessing that would be

for knowing God's will.
            But it doesn't work that way.

        What willpower
to accept the divine result of lots cast:
best two out of three, three out of five…

            and the High Priest looked at his watch
waiting till you like the result.

(I still have my official desk lamp
            purchased back then at the Co-op
to keep the school memory shining
            for my books and prayers.)

        Without divination stones
we wait, trusting nuance, referring to strength.
        We know (for Luke told us)

that the Spirit moves at God's speed,
            gets out ahead because alone
we'd be too slow
            to keep up or to see,
or too impatient
                to reflect, to turn,
to understand, to love.

*

Forty years ago,
            heartbroken
in a dream of silver bracelets,

        my farewell New England drive
left East Rock and crossed the place
            where the Mill and the Quinnipiac
                join New Haven Harbor
as I wound toward Mystic
            for no reason but to think.

        I had just returned

from the Knoxville World's Fair, 1982,
       two cars of us who decided
on a whim to spend the down time
         before graduation
    on a road trip, but I felt worse
than ever because
       I was going to miss these friends ....

And I had just called my friend Beth
      who lived back in Illinois,
to where I was returning
      because grad school plans had bombed.

     She'd just lost her husband
to cancer, and we talked, weeping,
      unsure about our respective futures,
but promising to be in touch soon,
     maybe over coffee once
I was back in a month.

    On my Mystic drive,
       I stopped at Branford,
and bought a New England picture book
     at a pharmacy
to cheer myself with a keepsake of

      the sweetest churches,
   weatherboarded homes and
       homes of stone,
fishing boats,
    and trees of red and gold
      shining in harbor water.

I thought how, in Bishop Ussher's scheme,
    Creation was an autumn week
and this must be the blessed vestige.

    Such a type of Eden
is New England, like the garden of the Oxbow
    that shone brightly
      in spite of storms.

For long years
        New England values
stood for the nation,
            values of liberty
                    and country
blessed for ongoing imagination,
        strong Pilgrims and their gratitude

            before so many were
                    lighting out for territory.

Marsden Hartley painted
            the rail fences of Connecticut
        beside the New Mexico mountains,

drawing distance together
        for the sake of land pristine for the moment,
            Edens of the West.

But stay true to the scriptures, wrote Timothy Dwight.

        Bless the Lord! and don't forget
            God's benefits, fierce providence
        for freedom through
all the bloodshed and mystery,

        remember God's care
            through all the years.

        a cleared wilderness and
New England liberty

            for all the wistful victors.

*

(There are story arcs
        of heritage and belonging
            as you draw distance

among Pangea's legacies,
while history's templates
                    crisscross and
stretch across centuries

as surely as poets
                echo from the long highways
through Israelite homelands

                    till we see God's justice
                        accomplished
                                for one and all.

Where are your places of kindness,
            and of love?

Where are you rooted?

Where do you belong?)

II

Light and Truth

New Haven, 1979-1982

Back then,
my friends and I were students of divinity
      as we lived in East Rock's sight
from our gradual hill.

      How the chapel steeple shone
bright like a psalm,
      golden hands like time's cherubim
        and the Celtic cross.

Truly, when the student is ready,
      teachers appear, friends,
crisscross journeys.

We lived and studied and kept
      ourselves on task, more or less,
pressed to soul-search.

Dearest friends, we knew
        Merton's prayer,
I've no idea where I'm going
      but recognized the voice:

Justice, justice you shall pursue...

If you knew me then, pen your name here:
      "I love you,_____."

Those were years of
      the deaths of Dorothy Day, Óscar Romero,
      and John Lennon.

      The four churchwomen
        raped and slain,
      disappearing Salvadorans—

our Cold War devastations.

Costly grace, agape and eros,
the love of study
and of subverting patriarchy,

all the while Christ pulled us in
like Caravaggio's Thomas
for flesh and blood.

(When we graduated, my mom
took a holy sip of blood,
thinking it was Welch's.®
She felt warmed heart and soul
by the sacramental red.)

Hugs and Midnight M*A*S*H,
Scripture's darker prayers,
the texts of the deep scholars

(and that friend who flung an impenetrable,
test-necessary text from the window
with a *Fuck you!*).

But drop the scriptures
and they cannot be broken.

If you love a place
where you cannot stay,

write your book with incidents
and insights
and northeastern leaves.

Love God, that ache.

*

Sometimes
we miss days of despondency
when they turn out indispensable.

In those days, I walked
all over—Harkness Tower,
Ezra Stiles, Cross Campus,
the High Street Bridge.

(Does the Tomb safeguard
Geronimo's skull?)

I searched for music,
felt my story as if in a pre-exilic tradition,
connections, contradictions,
warmed by flames of glory.

Around the Quad, millstones
were sunk for walking
too deep for one
whom Jesus warned about,
and too simple for a labyrinth,

more like a tree of life
on earth's surface, assurance
for the least of these.

*My sadness is greatest
in times of peace*, thus
St. Bernard. Maybe.

But I knew *Acquainted with the Night*,
embraced it above *Stopping by Woods*
in the little paperback
I bought up the road
from West Rock,

when Robert Frost took his flesh-thorns
for a walk

and pointed to Isaiah's Gospel
like the Baptist's skinny finger
toward the crucified Christ.

In God's seasons

there is a time for one thing
and a time for another.
        and back then,

it was time to study, to speak up,
        to write letters to family
            and to Congress,

            to minister
and keep community,

            to see what's playing at
Cinemas One through Infinity,

or cut over to Dixwell
        past the Winchester gun plant
            and north
to a restaurant in Hamden, or

catch Amtrak into the city, or

        wade through cool air to a friend's room
to visit, trade notes, or

        sing *The Wild Rover* with the Irish band
down by the harbor, or

        climb onto the roof
and work on tans and prayers,

        never mind the 55 degree day:
it's sunshine glorious,
            and it might not get so warm
        again till graduation,
even then it might rain
        like it did back in 1958.

Perhaps my red-haired Quaker buddy
        can meet for tea tonight.

And what sweet news

when the mail arrives
with Dad's homemade cookies,
        manna for all.

*

I had the Velázquez
        Christ Crucified
        on my wall at the desk—
he's very white,
        but those were the times—

my lifelong habit of something handy
                to remind me of faith,
        in case it drifts away
in short errands, fretfulness, and daily lists.

        (Today it's my Nicholas icon,
and Julian with her cat.)

        The Cross:
stationary wheel
        with Life at its center,

        Noah's gopher wood,
the shittim wood of the Ark,
        the Temple's Lebanon cedar:

        does God rescue with trees,
harvested for salvation?

        So much paper used
                in every Bible
and all that beauty,

        sun and stars for Torah,
flowers and rain for Prophets,
singing birds for Psalms and Writings,

        pleasant breeze and trees
for Gospels and Letters,

storm and rainbow for Revelation,
      a truthful road that is the Way.

I longed to learn what the ink
      showed me,
all those kings of Israel and Judah in order,
        and the tribes of Israel
    and where they settled both sides
      of the Jordan

and the way the Tabernacle looked
      and how Ezekiel's Temple looked,
and even how the End Times would be
    all laid out

and the tapestries of the Pentateuch
      and of the prophets
and the preaching routes of Paul

      and the forms of Christ
in the Old Testament

      and signs of God's kingdom
        in tangled, brutal times,

    and the assurance
that God opens his heart to all who turn to him,
    more than we can ask or think.

That nothing will ever close it.

    Nothing.

    *

One morning, I accompanied on piano
    the chapel service
of two black friends who preached
    in bright Marquand Chapel,
      morning light
from the high New England windows.

They read, *The Negro Speaks of Rivers.*

Dr. King expressed disappointment
    with white moderates,
and I was on a journey to do better,
    thankful to help. He knew:

freedom is a geography
    formed into shape
by faith and hope
    for all four directions,
        beauty of sound and love
from the waters of justice.

    (I didn't yet know that
        New England
was second home for Dr. King.
    Boston wove strands
in his tapestry:
    Coretta, his doctorate,
observation; his personal papers to BU;
    perhaps an ache for autumn leaves.

    He felt the call to ministry
        in Simsbury
working as a teenager at a tobacco farm,

    and felt astounded
to share restaurant meals with white folks
        in Hartford

while realizing there's much
    work to do.)

He wove in words:
    .... *"mountain of despair, stone of hope".*

*

The Tristan chord
    at Led Zeppelin level

                    from my dorm neighbor
musician buddy,
            helping me find

a lifelong love of Bach and Mozart,
                Vaughan Williams, Wagner....

            Remember our rolling production
for highway imagination
                with cassettes
in light fun of the PBS Boulez
            as we drove to Flagstaff:

            swimming saloon girls
by the headwaters,
                shining Walhall,
            saguaros that bloom though dry,
like Tannhäuser's staff.

            Music rings, and
Wotan *lights out for the territory,*
                half-blind across the Missouri
with his hard-riding
                    posse daughters
for a dreamed-of world

as the treaties he carves
            on his 1873 Winchester rifle
comes to cross purposes.

            Let Fricke, Erde reign instead,
women wise with justice,
                or Sieglinde her own hard-won wisdom,
spouse of her no-account rancher.

Promises to keep,
            for we know that threads are spun
and break, so we number our days.

            (Across the nation,
surely Elmer Fudd is on *someone's* TV

singing *kill the wabbit, kill the wabbit....*)

*

Students with books
          for a Labor Day afternoon
on our towels on warm sand at the harbor

          as East Rock in the near distance
was traprock to Heaven,
we passed around theologians' names
          like plates, health-giving ideas.

I was reading Karl Barth,
          stuck in the fine print, and
          one of us studied Greek,
another Hebrew—she was Presbyterian.

          Book after book caught sun
as waves managed the shore.

(I dream that the Reformers
          went to the beach,
Luther and his beer belly
                    pale in the sun, Calvin
          stern and systematic
when the beach ball hit him on the head

          as they searched
for God's mercies among
          doctrines made and lost
                    then preached for
a billion congregations.)

Time for a snack, and friends strolled across
the promenade to the stand's
          electric groove,

hair wet as I picture Christ's
                    at the Jordan,
          earth's water dripping
from the Lord of the waters

and blessing us as that day
we grew brown
      and read and dreamed,
the sand between our prayers.

*

      Heir to Edwards for those faithful
        who went forward
with a doable missionary theology
        and a brightened New England
        heritage.

New Haven Theology
      gave a historic hush
        to these brick columns
as we discerned spirits that are of God

in sought-out paperbacks,

      thinking someday I'd have
        a seminary office of my own
      in honor of profs who now
line halls in black and white.

      What a blessing to have
this green space for
      the Great Commandments
        among all our church traditions,

a place for bread and wine,
      ceremonies of belonging.

      Sure, Lessing said,
eternal destiny and historical events
      are unbridgeable,
a sad stop.

        But Tillich countered:
they correlate,
      don't lose hope,

you're accepted.

(I loved Tillich, first read
        in an Illinois service station
                where the family car

needed help, prairie expanse
        broken only by trees
                along the property lines,
Monopoly farm houses in the distance.)

        We all learned in 12 credits
that there is complexity and tension,
        in reading Scripture within our falling
and fallen cultures.

        But God's nature is relation,
is love,
        infinite love.

        Love mutes the brash cymbel
                and the loveless edicts.

Love says,
                jump!
        whether you're ready or set.

You learn, like Elijah,
        that there are ever pockets
of righteous people who love,
                so not despair.

You'll meet many of them.

        Some will mean the world to you.

        Some will never leave you.

*

        On an uneventful morning,

I made a happiness choice,
        a meal off campus,

not, this time, the IHOP® on Dixwell
        and the holy cheer of pancakes,

        but a weekend walk
down the hill, past the Chem building
        and the rink,

SOM and Silliman College and Old Campus

and shades of the Old Fence, of Handsome Dan
        barking at Harvard,

        to a restaurant somewhere along Chapel Street
where I had bacon with over-medium eggs

heavily salted
        for personal taste
(I was still young,
                screw it…)

with toast and butter,
        black coffee and OJ,

I ate and sighed,
                ate,
        thought a while,

                and looked at the back
the man in the next booth,
        his hair long, straight, and black
down his broad back.

        He explained his Native traditions
to the younger white man
        who listened and listened.

I didn't know there were Indians
        in New England,

I thought. What a fool.

I wonder now
        what he was saying to the white man.
I long to remember what he was saying.

But he was there,

and taught me, after all.

III

Metacomet

Flagstaff, 1987-1991

Five years after Yale—

    after her first husband died
        and we renewed our friendship
    and in God's bracing subtlety
        one thing led to another—

newlyweds Beth and I gained the grace
    of Flagstaff,
        four years
    for new teaching jobs,

    our daughter born there
on the eve of autumn,

our forever family link
        to this part
of Alta California

    and our Route 66 town
at the base of the San Francisco peaks,
        white-topped by October.

    God said, let there be
glory of ponderosas, the quaking aspen,
    firs and spruce,
        alpine tundra,

let Cambrian oceans
        wash the rocks,
    and let the sky be filled
        with western birds.

    We walked downtown
to shops with cloths of orange, blue, green and red,

healing crystals on chains of silver,

electric peace, a bell, a flute, a fetish:
        life-giver Kokopelli.

New England people, as it turns out,
        cut the titular staff and raised a flag.

This is land of Mogollon, Hohokam,
        and Ancestral Pueblo,
the Navajo, Hopi, and Zuni;

        Pima, Maricopa, Apache
            to the south;

Havasupai and Hualapai to the north
        and down the place
that needs words of both time and space—

        though they fail, too, when you stand
at the rim and gaze miles across
            those layered towers
        of infinite variety
            and so far down,

what we call the Colorado wearing away
        epochs of stone

of which Genesis has no record
        and yet makes me call upon
        that scripture's God
            as I close my eyes.

*

I'd never lived West,
        though I've distant lines
to the man who explored the Yellowstone
        and gave his name
        to Mount Washburn.

Moran painted a rainbow
>   in the park there, where the Nez Perce
>   ran for their lives…

If I could paint as Bierstadt
>   the Kaibab limestone
>   and Coconino sandstone,
>   old molten flow,

a 200-mile escarpment forming
>   the Mogollon Rim
>   of the Colorado Plateau,
I'd make devotion of the landscape
>   where I made quarterly drives

as Beth drove up
>   to Tuba City to teach

>   and I crossed that grand view
in the other direction

>   to a meeting
I'd no business attending—
>   Native American Ministries
>   down in Phoenix—

because nothing in my family history
>   earned me a place at that table—
>   slave owners, Indian haters—

except the assignment, and my kind heart to unlearn
>   the founders' fears:

O God, what have we done
>   *to deserve this mistreatment?*

What are your chastisements of love?

>   *as we've claimed these Native spaces*
as our own
>   *and they're no longer welcome—*

--my childhood on the Illinois prairie,
the richness
of glacial push and
unheard-of real estate,

land of my very being, true enough,
and of my parents and grandparents
and great-grandparents,

where Beth's and my ashes will
someday will be inurned.

*

(They say an ancestor of mine
was killed by Indians in central Ohio
on his way with his family
to the Illinois prairie

and his wife took the reins
to keep the children safe
before they continued on the National Road
in fear for their lives.

When was this? Around 1850,
twenty years after Jackson's
Indian Removal Act—

that tragedy for the Cherokee
which also relocated
the Seneca, Delaware,
Shawnee, Ottawa, and Wyandot
from Ohio in spite of the
Greenville Treaty

that had limited them far north
of my family's legend,
and years before 1850.

The tribes' caravans
stretched for miles

in November weather
                toward St Louis
                        and beyond,

their dead buried along the way,

another Trail of Tears
                forgotten by us

by most of us
                        whose family legends

embellish hostility rather than
                concern and regret for the tribes

                        for that is how we were raised.)

*

But I remembered the name Metacomet

and studied tribal traditions

                and learned them,
felt grateful when
                invited to the ceremonies.

                John the Baptist would scold me
                        to step up and
                do something worthy.
My poetry listens,
                        or tries to,
                will make mistakes and learn.

I'm of no tribe,
                with nothing to offer
a community
                        but respect,
                a humble heart.

I won't appropriate the traditions

as a well-meaning amateur,

or sample
        for my spirituality
that which gives *them* life and healing,

        or forget that my culture
has assaulted theirs
                and worse.

                New England, 1620-1676

*

And so, beside bay windows:
        my antique histories
for a Sunday afternoon,
                the grace of fresh coffee…

I imagine the violated quiet of Patuxet,

                and down water
beneath a sky of slate and orange

        the Mayflower,

not just one more English ship
        that the Wampanoags—
People of the First Light—
                had seen for so many years
        in the cold water,
even those ships that might have carried
        the Great Dying.

Forebear on board!
        His name was Francis Cooke, ancestor
of Grandma's Washburn mother.
                Heather Cooke
his wife came later, on the *Anne.*

        We didn't know all this

at the time of our big family thanksgivings
                    in Illinois

            at Grandma's house near Four Mile
Our family was Tolstoy in its own way,
me at the kids' table making
            mashed potato gravy reservoirs

                        even then urged to change,
subdue the landscape.

(Beth and I have been to Pieterskerk
                    and Leiden
        where the Puritans first stayed
for several years
            but faced fateful complications
before sailing out for more.

        How sweet there to hear
Vaughan Williams in my heart
                as we walked
        in Romanesque light:

the horn call of the Celestial City
        in a changing key,

        and modal pastures
where all the saints may pause
            before their rest
in D-major life,

        as if my English genes encoded
pilgrims' progress.)

On that boat, weary English
                with a newborn
affirmed freedom and self-rule
                for a common good
        and a common cause,

blessed sharing, a legacy blessed

to shape, to grow,
          refine, ever broaden, include,

then and through the years

      (though—whole truth—
Plymouth Rock weighed hard
      upon those who lived here already,
and those on other boats in chains).

In New England lived
      the Wampanoag, Narragansetts,
Mohegans, and others.
      Quinnipiacs at New Haven,
Pequots to the east at Mystic.

      Cooke's name stands out to me
on the Mayflower Compact.
      He served, owned land,
         hung out with Miles Standish,
lived to be quite old and lies on Burial Hill.

      Twelve years after the *Mayflower,*
      John Washburn
arrived in Plymouth,

leaving ten Worcestershire generations
      behind for the books—
         Evesham's Norman gateway
to the Avon Bridge,

the swallow's music
      at the church of Wichenford,
genetics from
         Plantagenet England.

John's son married
      a Cooke granddaughter,

and we genealogists have our field days.

*

There, I might've stopped.
        Genealogy does not always
prick the conscience,

                but the Native committee members
inspired me to go on,
        and in our own time to learn of

        murderous land destiny,
Native women disappeared,
        stolen lives in the Indian schools,

                each school with its own graveyard,

                unemployment's
        dogged sorrows, and the vagaries
                of the BIA.

                I repented as I could,
                        catching up on
        treaties broken,

the English longing to buy the land
that the Natives
                did not feel they themselves owned

                but traveled and used, unneedful of property deeds
or the permission of Kings James or Charles
                or any governor or president or Congress

                and on and on: Tippecanoe,
                        the Trail of Tears,

Lincoln's hanged Dakotas,
                Kit Carson against the Navajo,

                Sand Creek, Wounded Knee,
                        all the accounts that boast
                                of women, children, and elderly

slain. Elsewhere,

children were carried away
         to kill their Indian selves,
"education for extinction."

         What if your whole being
was perceived as a problem?

In old New England,
         could my Englishmen have started
                  a conversation?—

         People of the First Light,
we don't see reality the same
         yet we won't call that treason.

We do things differently
         but we can live at peace
one in God
         free in culture, sovereignty.

To offer you Christ will not be to destroy you.

         Jesus taught
to love one another,
         and wash feet and bind up wounds.

         Moses shows God's mitzvot
         to love the stranger,
                  to help the stranger
be secure as you would wish yourself …

         In theory, theology:
it wasn't impossible.

         But we breathe our cultures,
and people turn to war.

Eight million lay dead in Europe
         in those days

for religious crowns,
dry bones in armor across the fields,

stained glass eagerly smashed.

*

John Winthrop's sermon:
a city on a hill,

Christ's words through
Pilgrims and echoing down
    to Ronald Reagan
        and today
    and tomorrow,
witness of God, and of liberty,
    exceptional America.

(My father's folded casket flag
upon my shelves is a daily prompt.)

But let the exceptional name the violence,
      teach the wrongs,
    for the strong know metanoia.

It was Cain who built the first city
    a set place in the land of Wandering

and no children of Abel could come there
    to build homes, work,
      and love liberty.

The City runs risk,
as surely as the dark woman
    searched for her lover in the street,
was cat-called and lost her cloak.

Dream of God's city that is Peace,
    Shalom,
where there is freedom and goodness for all,
where freedom is built upon love

and rings from every town,

where war guns rust
        at the roadside,

        the city and the land
are continuous,
        and the name of streets
is the Healing of the Nations.

*

        Tisquantum,
Ousamequin met the Pilgrims,
        1621,
                signed a treaty with them
        and made possible
English survival, joined
        the Wampanoags to the Pilgrim side,

        on first face
                a potential benefit,
for the tribes had among themselves
                alliances and enemies,
sovereign cultures,
        and customs of brutality
to accept with a strong heart
        the silent spraying of your blood.

        (I remember my little grade school desk
in Illinois,
                with Elmer's® and crayons
for a Pilgrim hat of colored paper
        and red Indian masks,
                a turkey drawn
        from the fingers of my left hand,
my heart happy.)

        Knowing nothing
        but childhood lessons,
I thought I knew

the whole story

that day when I drove east
        toward Mystic and bought
that picture book

        but didn't seek the place of
the Pequot fort, 1638,
        the wall burned
under colonial command,

        Pequot women and children and elderly
were killed like combatants,

        as English and tribal enemies
rejoiced.

        Captain Mason declared:
Thus the Lord was pleased
        to smite our Enemies
in the hinder Parts, and to give us
        their Land for an Inheritance....

And Increase Mather:
Whole Companyes of them gathered
        and were burned to Death;
        those that escaped
        the Fire, the English
slew them with the Sword, so that round about
        the Fort, dead Men lay
hideous to behold.

        Mason's statue
                of appalling honor
        was at last moved to Windsor,
and tree of life planted

        at the circle site
and visible on satellite maps
        in files of ethnic cleansing.

Long after war, hearts changed:

How many intellectual beings
were hunted from the earth,
how many brave and noble hearts,
        of nature's sterling coinage,
where broken down
        and trampled in the dust.

*

        Promises to break

from the time of the first autumn,
        pragmatism and exegesis.

        Fuck you, I say to the title page
                of the book
that called the horror *entertaining*,

        though the book's
too antique and costly
        to pitch from the window

                and—hypocrite!—
how often throughout my life
                I've cheered
        the small-screen cavalry.

Let us make a hedge
                for God's protection

                the pilgrims said
        for the sake of our freedom of worship,
                beautiful and hopeful

yet, as if goyim English
                were Israelite,

and this space was reserved for Europe,
                freedom and belonging,

not to be shared

no matter the message
                of the fall moon.

*

        King Philip's War,

                miserable men
tortured, bodies covered by stone.
                        Severed heads along Eden's lanes.

Places of terror on both sides,
                women, children, old people killed.
                Rape.

                Bodies left behind
in the shade and swamp
                        after fearful retreats.

                My kin lived in Bridgewater,
which fared better

than towns by the dozen destroyed,
                Providence gone, Simsbury burned
                        to the ground. Settlements of

                the First Light peoples
                        ablaze, massacred.
                The Great Swamp,
                                Peskeompscut.

(More of my kin lived in Chelmsford,
                and lost a son.)

                Generations in trauma and
three anguished years
                                that set in motion

                killings and removal

for two centuries
till the frontier was closed.

Across New England, both sides could've cried:

we're planting, our children are playing.
We're being shot at.
They're shooting at us from the trees.

*

Col. Church gathered neutral Natives,
stalked like a champion
until, a watershed:

August 1676,
Metacomet died,
killed by a praying Indian,
his body face first in shallow water.

The body of Cromwell in England
and the body of Metacom in Plymouth
finally faired the same, hung dishonored
on poles, head
prominent and public.

Finally, captives
sailed off on other Mayflowers
to the south,
New England bound.

Finally, a treaty,
a deep breath before
the wars to come
as the French consolidate their own claims.

With a last New England glance,
shipped out to slavery,
the son of Metacomet might have said,

you compare scriptures left and right

till they tell you what you want,

that the sin of the father must be
visited on the son,
        for all of us are to you
            of the devil.

       Now, we feast each November:
for the Pilgrims needed
        the Wampanoags' help,

       a place to leave a myth
for our children's children.

*

       A hundred years,
And *savages* couldn't count
        toward in the Declaration's
          all men.

A hundred twenty years, and
        Washington served like Joshua
          as if Americans
    are Israelites in
empire exegesis,
        as Timothy Dwight rhymed
          in endless couplets.

Dwight rode all over New England
       for travel books
         and poetry, keeping fit

       when he wasn't looking after
the students of Yale, praying, writing
          for their faith, integrity.

He, too, saw New England
        as Canaan, a beacon of freedom and

righteous liberty worth the cost

for a nation's birth.

*

(Up in Bridgewater,

     forty years after the attacks,
a Washburn gave the land
         for the cemetery and meeting house
and buried his wife Rebecca there,
     1717,

     her grave was the first
and, eventually, all my Washburns
         of that time,
     their cared-for stones—

     effigies, sunbeam souls,
         and willow trees—

as yellow, orange leaves shade
     the gentle green.

So many bodies, white and red,
     went to earth
         without consoling places.

Mothers and fathers,
     your tangled, brutal times
         and mine,
     our lives in need of grace.

So many of your descendants
     were American public servants!

You prayed and risked and worked,
     died in hope,

and live in the genes
     of us millions.)

IV

A Pilgrim Son Retraces His Steps

This same Sunday afternoon
    at the bay windows,
        the grace of hot coffee:

story arcs of heritage and belonging,

    legacy.

    I remember the '60s,

    my father's library
of Western novels
    and Old West Time-Life books

toward the end of the Western's golden age

and my mom's favorite shows,
    when half our TV watching
was sheriffs and settlers,
    cowboys and Indians,

white actors in red face,

    and the fastest gun
brought justice.

  *

    I remember 1983,
Millstone Bluff in Little Egypt,

    Mississippian village remnants
and petroglyphs—Native Americans
    who moved of their own accord,
    a ghost memory

on the landmark hill

cherished by us much-later Anglos
        who sojourned
                into the deep-Illinois forest
        with its folks who, if you're blessed
to meet them,
        are dearest neighbors.

        On autumn day,
                a year after Yale,
Beth and I held hands on my parsonage porch
        as we gazed at the bluff—
                her engagement ring bright—

the year of the country birds of the field
        where I mowed around the oak and ash,
                the worry year of the Beirut barracks,

the year I played the Boulez excerpts
                of Wagner's *Ring*
        day after day after day,
then two days' wages splurged for Solti's set

        greedy as I was for filled hours
                at my Yale lamp,
my lonely waiting for *us.*

*

I remember when we moved to Flagstaff,
                1987, five years after Yale

and what a wonderful new start
        when we left the Saga Motel
                on old Route 66
once the moving van arrived, and till then

        there was nothing on TV
                but the Iran-Contra hearings

and MTV:
             U2 along the Glitter Gulch
as they searched for meaning
             in welcome, ringing gospel.

*

             (I remember a nearby motel on 66
                    and that man
who hadn't slept in a decent room
             for a week nor cleaned up

and found our church's phone number
             in the lobby's yellow pages.

      Three rows
             of steam-heated rooms with cable TV
for low prices were right
             so that folks
could have a warm bed.

      The trainee Good Samaritan

paid for his room, gave him
             a voucher for a meal—but he needed
friendship, a future,
             and I was afraid:

      my brother as surely as Christ
knew valleys and altitude,

      roads prepared for the Lord.)

*

I remember

      89A from Flag to Sedona,
forest forever damp, the rain on tourist cabins
             at roadside with rushing Oak Creek

ready for fishing, and sunny days
with the Navajo women and their jewelry
             spread on white linen at roadside:

country of Yavapai, Hopi and Navajo,
       Tonto Apache.

        Down the way,

hematite that stains red
       the Schnebly Hill grandeur,

harmonic beauty and our happiness
       beneath the Pedregosa Sea.

*

I remember Flag's daily gladness:

     the San Francisco Peaks,

     called by tribes by different names,
Nuva'tukya'ovi, Dook'o'oosłííd,

     while I, foolish, confused
Humphries and Agassiz
     from the south side…

     Years of faith's shock,
the catastrophic findings of Hutton, Lyell,

     that the earth was always as it is
now, and alters slowly, creating

uniform changes over epochs
     of which Genesis has no record.

Even Harvard master Agassiz--
     ichthyologist,
geologist, founder of glaciology,

could not step up
for Lyell's friend Darwin
   and his grandeur of life
     in our common origins,

the paradigm shift:
   selection explains
varieties of species,

   no more belief that
only whites claimed descent
   from Adam and Eve:

grandeur in the kinship
   of all people,
and all people with nature…

   Yet, not a social function,
not Darwin's wish to press
    natural selection
into a social philosophy

that's, frankly, evil—though Catlin,
    Remington put those notions

   to artistic work,
Social Darwinism in art,
   yet more wistful victors.

   In Arizona
    I learned so much,
and loved the sight of snow
   atop Mt. Agassiz
and its companions,

   sacred Hopi place
for new year and new life,
   the kachina spirits
who for blessing
    bring the rain.

*

I remember
      when friend Carol
          and her husband
visited us in Flag, 1989,

      one of our sweet reunions
          before she went on ahead.

      We all sat around the fireplace
          as snow fell on the Peaks
and Carol and I remembered
      seven years before when
she and I and our group drove down from New Haven
      to the Knoxville World's Fair.

I played for her the LP
      of those beloved Veracruz dances—

Huapango by Moncayo—

that had set to music the light show
      at the Mexican Pavilion.

      We laughed at the memories,
for what a silly, classic idea that had been,
          to make a sudden road trip
              with friends,
      divinity school Kerouac.

But Marguerite de Navarre knew,
      God helps those
          who go a little mad sometimes.

*

      I remember
when Beth and I made
      our third-trimester trip, 1990,
into the White Mountains,

near where Sitgreaves and his men
came exploring the Zuni, Little Colorado,
and Colorado Rivers

and had skirmishes with the Mohave—

our cabin room at Pinewood
as Beth and I read and gazed at the lake,
the strolling campers,
and her back hurt.

If I could paint in watercolor
the yellow wildflowers in the meadows
of Apache lands, cool waters
and Ponderosa Pines.

We took our time in Show Low
gift shops of turquoise, red, and gold,

drove down to the reservation,
then west along the forest road
of the soon to happen Dude Fire,

a stop in Payson,

then Montezuma Castle
to learn Sinagua culture

after a snack stop in Camp Verde

where that man and his burro
got ride-through lunch at Taco Bell®.

He joined a thousand family stories.

*

I remember eventful mornings

when the three of us set out north from Flag,
dear Route 180, 1991,

first to have breakfast
at El Tovar—

not for me, this time,
eggs heavily salted
            but French toast and coffee
        for two of us
and a bottle of formula for the other—

            while outside
        from the risen Kaibab limestone

            and the scaled-down clouds,
the handiwork of God and the Colorado

        that still nourishes the eleven tribes
and had for a very long time
            before Fred Harvey, Muir, and Powell.

        (My imagination runs out of breath
            on a hike down,

where I would be such a bright angel myself
            to know on sight
        strata, age, and stone,

        to know where to place my whole hand
on a billion years.)

*

        I remember our trips
south to Prescott, 1991, and that little
crossroad place at Humboldt
            and its own western peace

where I bought a Route 66 sign
            to cherish:
        Americans on the roads of flight
            and family adventure, postcards

of Native men on signs
        for Indian trading posts,
                small towns named out
        in King James cadence…

Now, his name won't stand out, but
        I love the writings of Alexander Humboldt,

so many places are named for him, though
        less common than Indian names,
                and his biographies grow.

Jefferson knew him, cherished him,
        welcomed him to the White House

        and tapped the Prussian master's
knowledge of the West and South,

        his true maps of New Spain
and geographic wisdom.

        Send information out
to Lewis and Clark, already mapping
        Louisiana.

        And there was Zebulon Pike,
whose plagiarized Humboldt maps
        gave him his own mountain fame.

        And there were the scientists
who followed him, Darwin, Wallace,
        Silliman, Bates, and Muir.

        And there were great Hudson River artists
who bring me back to New England
        and the West

called on Humboldt as their muse and blessing,

        and the great Southwest,
so beautifully described

in *Essay on New Spain* everyone read
and looked intrigued
             toward Alta California…

My copy of his book
             has someone's drawing
of the Battle of Veracruz,

             like a prophetic sign:

             America's drive for land,
coast to coast, in a hurry,

             "No time for Natives to adapt,
                          no time for the whites to feel remorse."

*

             (On both sides of Civil War,

Native men fought by the thousands
                          alongside the whites—
as they did in World War II.

             Paint them on panoramas
of Antietam, Second Bull Run, and Petersburg:

bravery for ancestral lands
                          they could regain,
             safeguard if,
perhaps, they could anticipate
                          the winning side

that would, in turn, honor treaties…

             though Reconstruction brought
few favors,

             and Sherman, Sheridan turned West
toward the tribes
             for that century's last decades

till the frontier was closed.

Across the Plains, the mountains,
        both sides could've cried:

        we're living, our children are playing.
                We're being shot at.
They're shooting at us from their horses.)

*

I remember four long days in cars,

2018, when the three of us and two cats
                set out from St Louis
for Tucson and Emily's masters degree
                in Asian studies:

        dear Route 66 scenes west
then down U.S. 70—"Broadway of America"—
                toward I-10
        in New Mexican enchantment;

        through
the Mescalero Apache reservation;

        the White Sands Missile Range
                and we waved bleakly toward Trinity;

stopped at Roswell, for gas and sodas and
little green souvenirs;

        the Thing;

and finally across to Tucson
                where on the mountainside
javelinas said hello.

A safe trip,
        new Arizona stories.

Kamisama, kansha itashimasu.

*

I remember in Arizona the beautiful cotton fields
       in Maricopa County,
acres of white brightening
       the unhuman, Arizona brown

          and I thought back
to Metacomet Ridge

      and days when I went out for
          a student's frugal twenty
along the trees of Whitney Ave

(for Eli Whitney is buried there in New Haven,
       near Noah Webster,
          like a dictionary cross-reference
of *cotton-gin* and *Manifest Destiny*).

*

Humboldt knew,
      as he charmed Silliman
          in perfect English
and feared America's
      penchant for aggrandizement,
          the extinction of the tribes.

We know:

burden the soil with a single crop
       like cotton
     and earth grows weary.

      Kill the animals and birds
         in waste
and they may not return.

Meet those who ask their food

forgiveness,
  and many will sneer.

Burn the forests, but only
  to renew the soil.

Cut the forests without love
  and the land suffers,
    the hills turn dry.

Learn to understand,
    to care,
  to see no shame in empathy,
      but shame in grounds for war.

Built-up land sinks to marsh,
  columns crumble.

  Empire's end point
can be forestalled with warning.
  So hoped Thomas Cole.

  Perhaps that was West Rock
that he showed in the background,
      the tenuous balance of
        a foundation stone.

  Perhaps his Oxbow
      was a warning, too:
that claimed and pretty Connecticut scene,
    with weather approaching
        that man cannot control.

And Moran painted it,
    slaves running through the dismal swamp,
the water oppresses,
    oppression ruins the earth,

cotton raised year after year
    so, more land must be taken
through slavery and through war.

And all those artists who painted scenes
in two versions,

blessedness and sin,

so, by the time of war, all the people
have taken sides, and the hills are shadowed,

America blood red
for the bright abyss
of Eden destroyed,

brush strokes of mourning
upon the paradise rocks.

Let our monuments remind, deter,
for little is settled by war,
only set up

for another, and another,
and another.

*

Native artists know,

sculpting shoreline shells
for treasured wampum,

praying toward the four directions.

The fire-lit cave walls
look like skin
as they provide shelter
on the Trail of Tears.

Pottery, jewelry, blankets, dance, and dolls,
photographs, film, poetry, prints, and prayer,
supporting collectives,
activism.

Our Diné blanket,
             sand paintings, wolf kachina,
                           and Wampanoag wampum

stir my Anglo heart

to learn whose land we're living on,
                 to learn all I can.

         To support sovereignty
                 and know their stories,

to urge memory places,
                              self-determination,

to ask how I can help.

         Remember that the continent
was not empty wilderness
         when the whites arrived
                 but was rich with language,
culture, values, spirits, contrasts, history.

         Remember the driven-out
and dead,
                 honor the mourning

and also see the celebrations,
         joy in family and the land.

Cherish honesty and respect,
                 restorative justice,

         the wisdom of women
                 and of elders.

Honor Earth,
         give back to her,
                 protect her.

Know that if man were gone,

she would thrive,
but not when man is hateful.

To all things, be kin.

*

William Apess, a Pequot, knew.
In 1836, he wove in words.

Lovers of liberty,
    let Metacomet
be remembered
    as the immortal Washington
is endeared in every white man's heart.

As with the jawbone of an ass
one nation has slain their brethren.

O thou pretended
hypocritical Christian, whoever
    thou art,
to say it was the design of God
    to murder and slay
  one another,
    to enslave a free people
and call it religion, virtue, when
the King of Heaven wills our power
    to serve the good of all.

Let every man of color
wrap himself in mourning
    on the day of the
  Mayflower's landing,
and on July the 4th.

Let the children of the Pilgrims
blush, while the son of the forest
    drops a tear and groans
    over the fate of his murdered
and departed fathers.

Let the white men
treat the colored people
    as human beings
before they go to convert any more,

    and tell it from the churches
and the housetops
    and pay the missionaries no more
        until they repent
    of their destruction.

God is merciful,
    and so his followers should be.
Has there been mercy for the Indians
    and their wives and children?
One example speaks for a thousand.

    You and I rejoice
that we don't have to answer
    for our father's crimes,
nor to charge them one to another.

    We can regret it, and flee from it,
and work for just laws,
    and let peace and righteousness
be written upon our hearts and hands
        forever.

Work must begin here first,

    in New England.

V

Written on Hearts and Hands

*

In time
my kin went West from Bridgewater:

leaving a trail of names,
biblical and Washburn, from

John and Elizabeth,
James and Mary,
                    Moses and Hannah,
Bezalel and Patience,

to David and Esther
who settled my hometown in Illinois
            in around 1830
                    and were buried
at timber's edge at Four Mile
            where my grandma's buried, too.

So many names, remembered
                    from plat books
and online files and histories
            of quarto size

as I dream the roadside trees
            and the fields
                    and the family stories.

I recite them
with my drive

when autumn paints colors,

when the timber turns cold and thistle-brown,

and when the green comes home.

*

(Grandma's grandpa Washburn
        lost his arm in battle, 1863,
                walked home to Four Mile

eager to see his young wife,
        only to find she'd died while he was away.

His was the 32nd Illinois,
        that saw action
at Shiloh, Vicksburg,
        Kennesaw Mountain, Atlanta,
and that long march to Savannah

when the land was throttled
        and railroads destroyed
and a thousand cotton gins
        smashed
                and civilians destitute,
a million and more bitter sorrows.

Elsewhere, the war
                devastated the Cherokees,
        another story, to go and learn.

We honored his local stone,
        simple, military, worn,

remembrance of war's hard hand.)

*

        When I was a boy, 1960s,
the Sunday highway led
        to Grandma's farm
10 miles east of town, near Four Mile,

        the day lilies, Queen Anne's lace

and switchgrass
	growing from the highway ditch hosting
yesterday's rain.

God said, let there be
	bur oak and black walnut,
maple and spruce,
	willows at riverside,

let the timber be bounded
	with honeysuckle, mulberry,
button bush
	with autumn olive,

let the bobwhite burst into startled flight,
	and the timber encircled
		by the dark birds.

	In the fields are
pumpjack wells,
	steel grasshoppers
rocked up and down

	for petroleum's worth,

twenty liters of oil a stroke
	from sandstone pools
of Pennsylvanian age along anticlines
	of this Illinois basin—

though not for us,
	1940s test wells on the back eighty
produced nothing,

		consequence of land claims
five generations ago
	for rich soil and timber beauty
as my kinfolk spent their days

	plowing, harvesting,
trading in town…

and for me,
as Thoreau could say, beloved lands

explored and tapped for words
        while the oil man thinks
he's the richer man.

*

I walked Grandma's acres
            in the warm seasons,

        the timber,
the place of the farm pond that
may still have cattails
        dragonflies and their nymphs
in the fresh water,

        the path of the cattle
became childish Indian trails,
        and I'd follow them.

        Her granary fence
was patched with the door
        of a '37 Chevy, lazy repair job and
my imagined gateway to childhood enterprise.

Fond branches of white ash,
        honeysuckle brush,
its bell-shaped corolla, creeping growth,

        pumpkins, gourds, strawberries,
her garden, her sickle
        a crescent moon,

always her African violets.

The three branches of Sand Run
        flow here, toward the river
by flowing toward Hickory Creek,
            and Overcup Creek in the south.

In winter, snow grew in the pastures,
    and the Christmas carols
   returned from the off-season
brightened the day's dull heavens
    across Vandalia's singing bridge.

*

   But this land is Native home,
confederation of the great Miami,
   Illini, the Kaskaskia River
    a tribal route.

Remember the story
   my ancestors told of a man
    who rode into town, around 1845—

even then a time when few whites
   had ever seen a Native man,
knowing only the trace of his stories—

and recalled his people, camps, villages,
   mounds from thirty years before.

   Now I live in St. Louis
where Osage, Miami, Sioux,
    and Iroquois thrived,

across the river is Cahokia Mounds
   of the great, lost city,

   and our Gateway Arch
    shares many stories.

*

   In those young days

Grandma gave me
   a Bible dictionary,

a present for a boy
        sort of interested, sort of not....

        But wait! Let a few years pass,
1979, and there I am
in divinity school, three years
        in sight of East Rock.

        The student is ready,
the books are at hand.
The books and their givers
                guided you!
                        Teachers,
cherished friends appear,
        crisscross journeys
over millstones for walking....

*

In a div school spring,
        when East Rock's winter purple fled,

        friend Paula and I
took "Daddy Stroble's" cookies

        and chatted together down the hill
for Bible class

where, thank God, we turned scripture around
        for plays of light.

How shall I know God?
        He judged the cause of the poor
and needy; then it was well.
        Is this not to know me? Says the Lord.

Shall I float, trusting God's current?
        But let justice roll down like waters,
and righteousness like an ever-flowing stream.

        Shall I travel the road

toward the Day of the Lord?

There will be a highway
    from Egypt to Assyria,
Egypt my people, and
        Assyria the work of my hands,
            and Israel my heritage.

Shall I pray that all shall know?
        strive first for the kingdom of God
and his righteousness,
        and all these things
            will be given to you as well.

What if, for all our searching,
        the meaning of life is clear?

He has told you, O mortal, what is good;
    and what does the Lord require of you…

        Justice, justice you shall pursue…

The city may be a sign
        of righteous visibility,

but the rainbow is the covenant sign,

        and its lights shine
as from the twelve stones
        in the breastplate of Aaron.

            Each is different,
        each has its special care,
            each has value
                    and each is the same
        in beauty, and beautiful together.

To love those treasured lights,
        and honor their needs,
    whenever you meet.

*

Abraham said,
>   *God will provide,*

>   *Deus providebit,*
Providence,
>   God's supervision and re-creation
>>   at every moment,
answering prayer or delaying response,

>   or consoling the grief-stricken,
>>   the victims
amid divine silence,
>   conferring blessing.

Drop the Scriptures, and they cannot be broken,
>   guiding us, consoling us.

>   Pick a psalmist,
whose cries of pain and fear to God
>>   is sacred Scripture.

>   Pick a prophet,
sorrowful at the spaces
>   where grace and free may border

>   but it's not yet clear.

>   Habakkuk
had his Job-like conversation with God,

>   questions of God and history,
>>   attitudes and actions
>   that set templates and

uncertainties across centuries—

>   till we see God's justice
>>   accomplished
>>>   for one and all.

*

The journey is a place of the Spirit,
and She nurtures us
          in places of belonging
                    upon the living earth.

Forty years ago,
          heartbroken and young,

          I made a farewell New England drive
across the place
          where the Mill and the Quinnipiac
                    join New Haven Harbor
as I wound toward Mystic,

and I bought a New England picture book
          at a pharmacy
as a keepsake of

                    the sweetest churches,
fishing boats
          and trees of red and gold
                    shining in harbor water.

I thought how, in Bishop Ussher's scheme,
          Creation was an autumn week
and this must be the blessed vestige.

(Over the years
          I lost the book
but found another, used, online—who knows,
                    it may be the same one.
          Trust God for subtlety.)

          Such a type of Eden
is New England,
                    like the garden of the Oxbow
          that seems to forestall
                    the clouds of storm.

For long years
        New England values
        stood for the nation,
                values of liberty
                        and country
blessed for ongoing imagination,
        strong Pilgrims and their gratitude

                before so many went West.

        But stay true to the scriptures, wrote the poet.
Bless the Lord! and don't forget
        God's benefits, fierce providence
        for freedom through
all the bloodshed and mystery,

        remember God's care
            through all the years.

Eden's words
            arc across chapters
        to the restored Tree of Life,

            the plentitude of water of life
that flows from the throne of God,
        bright as crystal
and waters the tree of life,
its leaves for the healing of the nations.

        In all our analogical Edens,
the wild branches forget,
        beloved of God forget

and push down the trees
        for freedom's sake,
one generation ruins something
        for the next.

Eternity takes time
        with puzzling strides,
        and we're apt to fill

                        the silent places
with selfish exegesis.

So, we pray,
            Lord, You have shown us what is good,

light us to study it, to do it,
            to perceive our scars of blindness.

A man appeared, grave and odd
            on the field of conflict
to Joshua, who said,
                        Whose side are you on?
and the man said, *Neither,*
            for I am from the Lord.

Listen! Wait for the Lord!
            before we're sure of everything.
Wait, it strengthens,
                        teaches nuance.

The movements of the Spirit
            work at the speed of God,

                        they get out ahead because
we'd be too slow
            to keep up or to see,

            or too impatient
                        to reflect, to turn,

            to understand, to love.

                                    New Haven, 2023

*

Beauty of the Metacomet Ridge,
            East Rock's
bold precipice of columnar basalt,
            crowned with trap, wrote Lyell,

90 meters above New Haven,

        chestnut oaks and red cedar,
diabase of brown and fractured scree.

Tremors of Pangea
        breaking—
                Africa, Europe, America,
move like Noah's nations.

        God said, let lava cool to tap rock—
what white men named New England—

        lithify, O sediment, to sandstone,
let erosion destroy so layers lift.

        God said, let the plants show
that life cannot be canceled,

        let them thicken into wilderness
                and be filled with eastern birds.

        How brighter
is East Rock's memorial
        than I remember,

visitors and hikers and children
        on a sunny afternoon.

        Below, our chapel steeple still shines,
bright as the psalm,
        golden hands like time's cherubim
            and the Celtic cross.

I'm in town again,
        an alumni fund board member
in my sharp suit,
        meals out with friends.

Down by Old Campus,
        that restaurant where I had breakfast once

is gone,

and the Native man in the next booth
        teaching his traditions

           to his young, Anglo friend.

But perhaps, somewhere,
        he is still teaching.

        We are here.

He teaches, still,
        the pilgrim son behind him.

*

Let peace and righteousness
        be written upon our hearts and hands
           forever.

Notes and Acknowledgments

Many thanks to Dr. Tom Dukes, who has made possible my dream of writing poetry. I appreciate friends Dr. Andrea Scarpino, Jane Ellen Ibur, Heathen, Maharat Rori Picker Neiss, Stacey Stachowicz and her family, Rev. Tweedy Sombrero Navarrete, Rev. Jason Bryles. Wonderful Yale Divinity School friends include James D. Hicks, Karen J. Allen, Tom Hannon, Dr. Joyce Mercer, Rev. Dan Appleyard, Dr. Julie Galambush, Rev. Julie Berger, Rev. Paula Ritchie, and also Emily DeLorenzo Reid. My dedicatee, Dr. Carol Thysell, was a YDS friend who died of cancer in 2001. I also appreciate the Webster Groves Starbucks, the Novel Neighbor Bookstore, the St. Louis Poetry Center. Most of all, I appreciate Beth and Emily and our cat buddies!

To write reflectively about one's family history, when it includes chattel slavery and warfare against Native Americans, may provide a very small gesture toward justice that, one prays, God may use for good. The words of William Apess, quoted herein, are instructive for acknowledging the past, listening to other voices besides our own, and working for the present and the future. I hope some of the works cited below are helpful, as they were for me.

This work continues an earlier book, *Walking Lorton Bluff* (Georgetown, KY: Finishing Line Press, 2021) as a project to reflect on my own ancestry with certain justice issues in mind. This work also continues my book, *Four Mile* (Georgetown, KY: Finishing Line Press, 2022). Several poems herein (or portions of poems) first appeared in *Four Mile*. For several years I've been exploring the sense of place in some of my books and blogs.

These poems go back and forth and around in place and time, so it may be helpful to say: I was a student at **Yale Divinity School** in 1979-1982, ("forty years ago"), about which I write in Section I and especially Section II.

Two years after I graduated, Beth and I were married. We attended grad school together and lived in **Flagstaff, AZ** in 1987-1991. I wrote about these years in Sections III and IV.

My ancestor Elizabeth Mitchell (1629-1684) was the granddaughter of Mayflower passenger Francis Cooke (1583-1663). Elizabeth married John Washburn (1620-1686), who emigrated to Plymouth Colony from Bengeworth in 1635. They lived in **Bridgewater, MA.** Four of their sons participated in the bloody King Philip's War (1675-1676). I write about the war in Section III, a musing inspired by Native American pastors whom I knew in Arizona.

John and Elizabeth's great-great-grandson David Washburn went West in about 1830 and settled an area called **Four Mile**, east of Vandalia, IL. I was born and raised in Vandalia.

My grandma Grace Crawford lived near Four Mile. It is through Grandma that I'm descended from these Washburns. She figures briefly in Section III and strongly in Section V. She was a great influence on me to attend Yale Divinity School—though I didn't know at the time that we had such deep roots in New England.

I

"Forty years ago...." On the geology and art of East Rock, see Jelle Zeilinga de Boer, *Stories in Stone: How Geology Influenced Connecticut History and Culture* (Middletown, CT: Wesleyan University Press, 2009) 125-130.

"The ridge is no geography...." On Silliman, see de Boer, 114-115. Benjamin Silliman (1779-1864) was one of America's first professors of science. He was hired by Timothy Dwight to teach at Yale, in 1804. Silliman was the first in America to use factional distillation. He also founded the *American Journal of Science*, which has been published since 1818. As I write about in section IV, he and Alexander von Humboldt met one another in Berlin in 1851.

"But there's a story arc..." Julie Galambush, *Reading Genesis: A Literary and Theological Commentary* (Macon, GA: Smyth & Helways Publishing, Inc, 2018): "Each human life manifests God's presence, and for that reason, each human life is sacred ([Genesis] 9:6) 22. Also, the chapter "Perek Alef: Why does so much of such importance in Jewish history happen in the Midbar—in the Desert?" in Harvey J. Fields, *A Torah Commentary for Our Times, Volume Three: Numbers and Deuteronomy* (New York: URJ Press, 1993) 9-13.

"If I could paint in Hudson River style...." Jelle Zeilinga de Boer and John Wareham, *New Haven's Sentinels: The Art and Science of East Rock and West Rock*. Middletown, CT: Wesleyan University Press, 2013. Part of this poem first appeared, in a different form, in my poetry book *Walking Lorton Bluff*. Georgetown, KY: Finishing Line Press, 2019.

"The grand, granite pedestal...." "Connecticut's Civil War Monuments, New Haven, Soldiers' and Sailors' Monument," https://chs.org/finding_aides/ransom/074.htm. Accessed December 14, 2022. The monument honors New Haven soldiers and sailors of the Revolutionary War, War of 1812, Mexican War, and Civil War.

"Across the valley..." Three "regicide judges"—judges who had signed King

Charles I's death warrant—fled to Boston in 1660. They were John Dixwell, William Goffe, and Edward Whalley. During the summer of 1661, Goffe and Whalley hid at a rock shelter near New Haven now called Judges Cave. Dixwell died in 1689 and is buried on the New Haven Green, while the fates of Goffe and Whalley are undocumented. Goffe, however, is the focus of the "Angel of Hadley" legend when he is said to have appeared and encouraged the English when Hadley, MA was under attack from Native tribes in 1675. Three New Haven streets are named for the judges.

On Goffe's purported appearance, see Eric B. Schultz and Michael J. Tougias, *King Philip's War: The History and Legacy of America's Forgotten Conflict* (New York: The Countryman Press, 1999) 228-232. As the authors discuss, Stiles embellished the story that had first appeared in another work. Earlier authors like William Hubbard and Increase Mather had not reported it.

Ezra Stiles' book is *A History of Three of the Judges of King Charles I. Major-General Whalley, Major-General Goffe, and Colonel Dixwell: Who, at the Restoration, 1660, Fed to America; and Were Secreted and Concealed in Massachusetts and Connecticut, for Nearly Thirty Years. With an Account of Mr. Theophilus Whale, of Narraganset, Supposed to Have Been One of the Judges.* Printed by Elisha Babcock, Hartford, 1794.

"Legend was that Ezra Stiles…" Ezra Stiles (1727-1795) was Yale's seventh president (1778-1795). He wrote a book about the regicide judges, as well as other works. He also made important notes on the New England landscape, including sites from King Philip's War.

On Ezra Stiles' presidency, see Reuben A. Holden, *Yale: A Pictorial History* (New Haven: Yale University Press, 1967) 14. Ezra Stiles did not, as once thought, choose Urim v'Tummim for Yale's shield. His own Yale diploma shows evidence of its earlier use.

"Forty years ago, heartbroken…" David Gibbon, New England: *A Picture Book to Remember Her By.* New York: Crescent Books, 1979. On the values of New England (and the Marsden Hartley painting), see Julia B. Rosenbaum, *Visions of Belonging: New England Art and the Making of American Identity.* Ithaca, NY: Cornell University Press, 2006. This book was an early inspiration for these poems.

Yale's eighth president, Timothy Dwight (1752-1817) succeeded Ezra Stiles and served in 1795-1817. That section "But stay true…" is inspired by from Timothy Dwight, "An Address, to the Emigrants from Connecticut, and from New England Generally, in the New Settlements in the United States". Hartford: Printed by Peter B. Gleason & Co., 1817.

Dwight wrote the first epic poem in America, *The Conquest of Canaan*

(1785), in which he parallels the biblical narrative of the slaughter of Canaanites in the book of Joshua, with the genocide and displacement of Native tribes in the establishment of America. Though he didn't live to see it, Dwight had the idea to establish a divinity school at Yale, which I attended in 1979-1982—"forty years" ago, as I put it in this poem (written in 2022). Yale Divinity School celebrated its two-hundredth anniversary in 2022.

II

"Back then, my friends and I ..." Merton's prayer is easily found online and was first published in Thomas Merton, *Thoughts in Solitude.* New York: Farrar, Straus and Giroux, 1956. The scripture "Justice, justice you shall pursue" is Deuteronomy 16:20.

I received permission from the friend to use the story of her tossing the textbook.

"Sometimes, we miss..." The scripture "if it be not so...." is Daniel 3:18. The scripture "A bruised reed..." is Isaiah 42:3.

The poem mentions a labyrinth: today, there is a labyrinth on the YDS campus, next to Marquand Chapel.

"I had the Velázquez..." Part of this poem was first published in my poem *Four Mile.*

"One morning, I accompanied on piano..." I intended for Dr. King's justice work in New England to echo, if subtly, William Apess' calls for justice and righteousness in his "Eulogy for King Philip," page 74 of this poem. See, for instance, Elisabet Engsbråten, "The Dream and the Looking-Glass: Race and Rhetoric in William Apess and Martin Luther King," A Thesis Presented to the Department of Literature, Area Studies, and European Languages, 30-Point Thesis, University of Oslo, In partial Fulfillment of the Requirements for the MA Degree, Spring 2017. https://www.duo.uio.no/bitstream/handle/10852/57927/Engsbra-ten_MA.pdf?sequence=1&isAllowed=y. Accessed January 24, 2023.)

My lines "freedom is a geography... the waters of justice" were suggested by or echo Dr. King's "I Have a Dream" speech, while "mountain of despair, rock of hope" come from that speech.

On Dr. King in New England, see Doug Most, "The Ways Boston Helped Shape the Life of Martin Luther King, Jr. (GRS'55, Hon.'59)", Bostonia: Boston University's Alumni Magazine. January 22, 2019. https://www.bu.edu/articles/2019/mlk-boston/. Accessed January 21, 2023; "MLK Remembered His Time in Simsbury Fondly", January 20, 2020 (originally published in 2012).

https://www.nbcconnecticut.com/news/local/mlk-remembered-his-time-in-simsbury-fondly/2212132/. Accessed January 21, 2023.
"The Negro Speaks of Rivers" is, of course, Langston Hughes' beautiful poem.

"Students with books ...." Another version of this poem was published in my book *Walking Lorton Bluff.*

"On an uneventful morning..." The July 2022 issue of *National Geographic* is titled, "North America's Native nations reassert their sovereignty: 'We are here.'" Because he was "there", the man in the restaurant alerted me of my ignorance of Native Americans in New England. The wistful myth of the noble but doomed, "vanishing Indian" is very strong. But to linger in that myth is to neglect understanding how tribes have preserved their culture and language, pushed for honored treaties, and promoted sovereignty—and still do. Years later, my memory of the man inspired this pilgrimage into family history and Native American heritage.

Tocqueville himself, erroneously, believed that Indians were extinct in New England: "None of the Indian tribes which formerly inhabited the territory of New England, --the Narragansetts, the Mohicans, the Pequots--have any existence but in the recollection of man." Alexis de Tocqueville, *Democracy in America.* Translated by Henry Reeve, Esq. Third American Edition (New York: George Adlard, 1839) 335.

A fascinating book is by Pekka Hämäläinen, *Indigenous Continent: The Epic Contest for North America.* New York: Liveright Publication Corp, 2022. A dominant perspective of American history focuses upon settlement by those of European descent. Hämäläinen provides a counterbalancing view: that Indigenous peoples continued to thrive and flourish through the late 1800s. While the French and British were "removed" from the American continent, Indigenous populations were not victims of an inexorable destruction, though they certainly suffered death, tragedy, and removal over the decades. America can be called an "Indigenous continent" because Native Americans long remained at or near the center of social policy and U.S. history. The Native American nations, of course, continue, and their people still press for their well-being, sovereignty, and land repatriation. Writing in *The New Yorker,* Ojibwe author Davie Treuer writes that Hämäläinen's view is helpful for him, having read the more elegiac *Bury My Heart at Wounded Knee* as a college student (Nov. 14, 2022, 73-76).

III

"Five years after Yale...." The Native American Ministries meetings that I attended were led by Rev. Harry Long and Rev. Tweedy Sombrero. Rev. Long was a Muscogee Creek Indian of the "Wotko" or Raccoon clan and a United Methodist minister, and Rev. Sombrero Navarrete is a Diné (Navajo) pastor in the United Methodist Church, one of the first Native women to be ordained. I'm grateful how they welcomed me to the meetings.

"I'd never lived West…" A major experience in the Native American history in Illinois was the Black Hawk War in 1832. Governor John Reynolds called up the state militia to deal with Black Hawk and his people. Three of my relatives participated in the war, one of whom, John A. Wakefield, wrote the first history of the war, making the case for what he considered the rightness of Reynolds' action. Wakefield was my first cousin by marriage five times removed.

"(They say an ancestor of mine…" I refer here to my 3rd-great-grandfather Paul Crawford, a descendant of Scottish immigrants and whose grave is marked: https://www.findagrave.com/memorial/153835052/paul-crawford Accessed October 19, 2022. Also: Jim Blount, "What happened to Indians that once inhabited Ohio?" Historical Collection at the Lane, 2017. https://sites. google.com/a/lanepl.org/columns-by-jim-blount/home/2017-articles/what-happened-to-indians-that-once-inhabited-ohio. Accessed October 22, 2022.

"But I remembered the name Metacomet…." See this story about the Wampanoag tribe: Paul Grant-Costa, "We did not land on Plymouth Rock. Plymouth Rock landed on us." Op-Ed: the blog of the Yale Indian Papers Project, November 24, 2016. https://campuspress.yale.edu/yipp/we-did-not-land-on-plymouth-rock-plymouth-rock-landed-on-us-2/. Accessed October 24, 2022. (The title of the op-ed comes from Malcolm X's speech in Washington Heights, NY, March 29, 1964, when he famously said, "Our forefathers weren't the Pilgrims. We didn't land on Plymouth Rock; the rock was landed on us."

I have enjoyed Randy Woodley, *Becoming Rooted: One Hundred Days of Reconnecting with Sacred Earth*. Minneapolis: Broadleaf Books, 2022. Woodley writes that he is a Cherokee descendant recognized by the Keetoowah Band of Cherokee but was not raised in Native American culture, coming to it in his twenties.

"And so, beside bay windows…" See Nathaniel Morton, *New-England's Memorial, or, A brief Relation of the most memorable and remarkable Passages of the Providence of God, manifested to the Planters of New-England, in America: With special Reference to the first Colony thereof, called New Plymouth*. Newport: Reprinted, and sold by S. Southwick, 1772. The book first appeared in 1669. Morton was the first to publish the content and signers of the Mayflower

Compact (a document which no longer exists), as well as the story of the first Thanksgiving.

My sites https://paulstroble.wordpress.com/2014/08/04/my-family-the-washburns-back-to-the-pilgrims/ and https://paulstroble.wordpress.com/2017/06/01/the-washbourne-family-in-england/ provide some genealogy about the Washburn family, their connection to Francis Cooke, and their English heritage.

Regarding Pieterskerk (Peter's Church in Leiden, where the Pilgrim community worshiped prior to their departure for North America): the music to which I refer is a favorite piece, Ralph Vaughan Williams' Symphony #5, which contain several of RVW's associations with Bunyan's *Pilgrim's Progress*, a book that eventually he turned into an opera. It is wonderful that the website of the historic church contains both the Pilgrim and the Native American sides of the Thanksgiving story: https://pieterskerk.com/en/museum/pilgrims-exhibition-history/

At least five of the eight children of my ancestors Francis and Hester Cooke were born in Leiden, including their daughter Jane from whom I'm descended.

"There I might have stopped..." On the bloody European history contemporaneous with the Puritans (who are, of course, also Europeans living in a European colony), see, for instance, John Matusiak, "A conflict beyond peacemakers: James I and the Thirty Years' War." The History Press, https://www.thehistorypress.co.uk/articles/a-conflict-beyond-peacemakers-james-i-and-the-thirty-years-war/ . Accessed August 8, 2022.

On the terrible institution and legacy of boarding schools, see, for instance, David Wallace Adams, *Education for Extinction: American Indians and the Boarding School Experience, 1875-1928*. Lawrence: University Press of Kansas, 2020; Alexandra E. Stern, "Reconstructing Approaches to America's Indian Problem, Indian Policy in the Late Nineteenth Century." U.S. History Scene. https://ushistoryscene.com/article/usindian-policy/. Accessed October 6, 2022; and "Each School Had a Graveyard: Native American Boarding Schools." Civil Rights Teaching. https://www.civilrightsteaching.org/each-school-had-a-graveyard. Accessed October 6, 2022.

On Native American impulse to war, author S. C. Gwynne commented on the NPR show Fresh Air, "there was … an attempt at one point to deny that Indians were warlike. Comanches were incredibly warlike... [I]f you look at the Comanches and you look back in history at Goths and Vikings or Mongols or Celts—old Celts are actually a very good parallel. In a lot of ways, I think we're looking back at earlier versions of ourselves. We—being white European—did all of those things. Not only that but torture was institutionalized during things like the Counter-Reformation and the Spanish Inquisition and the Russian Revolution." Author interviews, "The Rise and Fall of the Comanche 'Empire'", posted May 20, 2011. https://www.npr.org/2011/05/20/136438816/ the-rise-and-fall-of-the-comanche-empire. Accessed October 6, 2022. See also Hämäläinen, *Indigenous Continent*.

In her book, *The Name of War: King Philip's War and the Origins of American Identity* (New York: Alfred A. Knopf, 1998), Jill Lepore explains how the English settlers of New England engaged in savage acts while self-consciously struggling not to become like the Indians whom they condemned as "savages."

"In theory, theology...": I mean by that, the biblical doctrine of sanctification, the power of God to transform people in love and service. But in their own spiritual journeys, the English in New England viewed themselves as God's people at war with forces of Satan. This partly explains the savagery of, for instance, the Mystic Massacre of the Pequots in 1637. And in Native culture of the time, violent reprisals were necessary to maintain the world's spiritual balance—for the world was alive with spirits. Ron Rosenbaum, "The Shocking Savagery of America's Early History," an interview with historian Bernard Bailyn, author of esteemed works of early American history. Bailyn also notes that the rules of chattel slavery was set in America by the end of King Philip's War. *Smithsonian Magazine*, March 2013. https://www.smithsonianmag. com/history/the-shocking-savagery-of-americas-early-history-22739301/. Accessed December 29, 2022.

"John Winthrop's sermon..." His 1630 sermon uses Jesus' phrase "a city on a hill" to call attention to God's expectations for Massachusetts Bay Colony: it should be an example to all. https://www.americanyawp.com/reader/colliding-cultures/john-winthrop-dreams-of-a-city-on-a-hill-1630/ Accessed February 8, 2023.

See, also, Donald M. Scott, "The Religious Origins of Manifest Destiny, TeacherServe, May 4, 2022. https://nationalhumanitiescenter.org/ tserve/nineteen/nkeyinfo/mandestiny.htm. Accessed August 13, 2022. Scott writes, " 'Manifest Destiny' became first and foremost a call and justification for an American form of imperialism, and neatly summarized the goals of the Mexican War... 'Manifest Destiny' was also clearly a racial doctrine of white supremacy that granted no native American or nonwhite claims to any permanent possession of the lands on the North American continent and justified white American expropriation of Indian Lands..." Scott traces the origins of this imperialism in the Providential purpose that the New England Puritans brought with them to the continent as they sought a place of freedom, freedom of worship, and devotion to God. He notes that Winthrop does invoke

Micah 6:8 as a feature of the city on the hill. But in the decades that followed, the travails of the settlers—including warfare with the Native tribes, accusations among settlers of witchcraft, as well as difficult weather—refocused the settlers from being exemplary to the possible reasons why God might be chastising them for faithlessness. This providential theology, Scott notes, was very strong in the Civil War era and permeated Lincoln's second inaugural address.

The words "The City tempts" alludes to Song of Songs 5:6-7.

"Tisquantum, Ousamequin met the Pilgrims, 1621, …" These are the proper names of Squanto and Massasoit.

Sixteen years after English settlement began in New England, on May 26, 1637, English forces under Captain John Mason, and their Mohegan and Narragansett allies, burned the Pequot Fort at Mystic, killing hundreds of Pequot civilians. Historians note that the war was the first example of "total war" in the new world. See, for instance, *A brief history of the Pequot War: especially of the memorable taking of their fort at Mistick in Connecticut in 1637: / Written by Major John Mason, a principal actor therein, as then chief captain and commander of Connecticut forces; With an introduction and some explanatory notes by the Reverend Mr. Thomas Prince.* Printed & sold by. S. Kneeland & T. Green in Queen-Street, 1736. Reprinted by J. Sabin & Sons, New York, 1869. The quotation is from the Sabin reprint, page 18.

I slightly condensed the Increase Mather quotation, which is from his *Early History of New England Being a Relation of Hostile Passages Between the Indians and European Voyagers and First Settlers: and a Full Narrative of Hostilities, to the Close of the War with the Pequots, in the Year 1637: Also a Detailed Account of the Origin of the War with King Philip.* With an introduction and notes by Samuel G. Drake (Boston: Printed for the Editor, 1864) 171.

The quotation, "How many intellectual beings…" is by Washington Irving and quoted in Schultz and Tougias 33.

"Promises to break…" Thomas Church, *The entertaining history of King Philip's War, which began in the month of June, 1675. As also of expeditions more lately made against the common enemy, and Indian rebels, in the eastern parts of New-England: with some account of the Divine Providence towards Col. Benjamin Church: / By Thomas Church, Esq. his son.* Boston: Printed, 1716. Newport, Rhode-Island: Reprinted and sold by Solomon Southwick, in Queen-Street, 1772.

In 1675-1678, King Philip's War was proportionately the deadliest war in American history. Native tribes, frustrated with English encroachment and broken agreements, attacked and burned many villages. English forces attacked many Native settlements, including the Narragansett fort at the Great Swamp in Rhode Island. The death of Metacomet by another Native was essentially the end of the war, in 1676, although a treaty was signed in 1678. Metacomet's head was displayed on a pole at Plymouth for many years. His family was sold into slavery.

George Madison Bodge, *Soldier's in King Philip's War* (Boston: Printed for the Author, 1906), lists my 7th-great-uncles John and Jonathan Washburn of Bridgewater, MA (pp. 428, 458). Find-a-Grave adds their brothers Thomas and Samuel as also participating. They and their brother James, my direct ancestor, are buried in Bridgewater's First Cemetery.

Recent histories of the conflict include Lepore; Schultz and Tougias; Douglas Edward Leach, *Flintlock and Tomahawk: New England in King Philip's War.* Hyannis, MA: Parnassus Imprints, Inc, 1958; Lisa Brooks, *Our Beloved Kin: A New History of King Philip's War.* New Haven: Yale University Press, 2018; Christine M. DuLucia, *Memory Lands: King Philip's War and the Place of Violence in the Northeast.* New Haven: Yale University Press, 2018.

The metaphor of the "hedge" is discussed by Peter N. Carroll in his book, *Puritanism and the Wilderness: The Intellectual Significance of the New England Frontier, 1629-1700.* New York: Columbia University Press, 1969.

"Vast nomenclature": see Lepore 238-239.

On Metamora, see Lepore 191-226. John Augustus Stone's play based on Metacomet was titled *Metamora; or, The Last of the Wampanoags* and premiered in 1829. The play was very popular during the antebellum era, so much so that towns in four states were named after the play. Lepore discusses how the historical distance between Metacomet and "Metamora" allowed for sympathy among white audiences for the defeated sachem. He was by no means "the last Wampanoag", but the designation dovetailed with the myth of the vanishing Indian. Because the Indian Removal Act, so devastating for the Cherokees, took place at about the same time as the play, Lepore argues that the play was a milestone in American identity, advancing the cruel notion that Indian removal was unavoidable (224).

"King Philip's War…" In addition to the sources cited above, see Lepore 71f; Robert E. Cray, Jr., "Weltering in Their Own Blood": Puritan Casualties in King Philip's War," *Historical Journal of Massachusetts,* Vol. 37(2), Fall, 2009:106-123. https://www.westfield.ma.edu/historical-journal/wp-content/uploads/2018/06/Weltering-in-their-Own-Blood-Puritan-Casualties.pdf. Accessed Aug. 8, 2022.

Also, William Hubbard, *A narrative of the Indian wars in New-England, from the first planting thereof in the year 1607, to the year 1677: Containing a relation of the occasion, rise and progress of the war with the Indians, in the southern, western, eastern and northern parts of said country.* Boston: Printed and sold by John Boyle in Marlborough-Street., 1775. First published in 1677. Reflecting the providential theology of the Puritans, Hubbard comments about my ancestors' community: "Not long after, May 8th [1676], they burned about seventeen houses and barns in Bridgewater, a small town in Plymouth colony, twelve miles on this side Taunton; but it pleased God just at the time to send a thunder-shower, which put out the fire, or else it might have prevailed much further. It is very remarkable, that the inhabitants of the said Bridgewater, never yet lost one person by the sword of the enemy, though the town is situated within Plymouth colony, yet they have helped destroy many of the enemy. None knows either love or hatred by all that is before them in things of this nature; nor ought standers[-]by that may escape, think themselves less sinners than those that perish by the sword of the enemy: Yet about this time four of the inhabitants of Taunton were killed as they were at work in the field, whereby it is said thirty children were made fatherless: So unsearchable are the judgments of the Almighty and his ways past finding out" (171).

The Washburns are on my mother's side. On my father's side, my 8th-great-grandfather Edward Colburn (1618-1700) built a Garrison House in Chelmsford, MA to defend himself and his family from Native attacks during the war. Edward was born in Cornwall and emigrated to the Massachusetts Bay Colony in 1635, traveling on the Defense. One of his sons, also named Edward—my 8th-great-uncle—was killed in an ambush by the Nipmuc tribe on August 2, 1675, an incident known thereafter as Wheeler's Surprise. This family also appears on Find-a-Grave.

"Col Church gathered…." The phrase "New England bound" is from Wendy Warren, *New England Bound: Slavery and Colonization in Early America*. New York: Liveright/W.W. Norton, 2016.

There are many works on the "myth" of the first Thanksgiving, so precious for many of us even when we know its romanticized nature. See, for instance, "Thanksgiving Fairy Tale and Myth," Nov. 26, 2015. http://court. rchp.com/thanksgiving-fairy-tale-and-myth/. Accessed August 13, 2022. Also: David J. Silverman, *This Land Is Their Land: The Wampanoag Indians, Plymouth Colony, and the Troubled History of Thanksgiving*. London: Bloomsbury Publishing, 2019.

"A hundred years…." The Declaration of Independence, with its foundational phrase "all men are created equal," nevertheless describes the tribes: "He [King George] has excited domestic insurrections amongst us, and has endeavored to bring on the inhabitants of our frontiers, the merciless Indian Savages whose known rule of warfare, is an undistinguished destruction of all ages, sexes, and conditions" (Grievance 27).

On Timothy Dwight, see his books, *Travels in New England and New York*. Four volumes. New Haven: Published by Timothy Dwight, S. Converse, printer, 1821; and also Timothy Dwight, *The Conquest of Canaan: A Poem, in Eleven Books*. Hartford, printed by Elisha Babcock, 1785. Also, Bill Templer, "The political sacralization of imperial genocide: contextualizing Timothy Dwight's *The Conquest of Canaan*." https://doi.org/10.1080/13688790600993230. Accessed August 2, 2022.

"(Up in Bridgewater....)" The site findagrave.com provides many of the burials in Bridgewater's First Cemetery.

Among descendants of these Washburn settlers are numerous politicians and holders of public office. See https://fascinatingpolitics. com/2021/02/10/the-washburns-a-most-influential-family/comment-page-1/ and https://en.wikipedia.org/wiki/Washburn_family. Both accessed October 6, 2022. Noted 19th-century statesman and diplomat Elihu B. Washburne is among them.

IV

"This same Sunday afternoon..." "Land acknowledgements honor a place's Indigenous people—past and present—and recognize the history that brought us to where we are today. They are meant to recognize how we have inadvertently benefited from the history of colonization, removal, and genocide of Indigenous people. Land acknowledgements are a starting point. They should not be the only way you recognize or support Indigenous communities and histories." Kathryn M. Buder Center for American Indian Studies. https://sites.wustl.edu/budercenter/land-acknowledgment-2/. Accessed August 16, 2022. See also "Analysis: How well-meaning land acknowledgements can erase Indigenous people and sanitize history," PBS News Hour, Oct. 10, 2022. https://www.pbs. org/newshour/nation/analysis-how-well-meaning-land-acknowledgements-can-erase-indigenous-people-and-sanitize-history Accessed March 8, 2023.

"I remember 1983, Millstone Knob in Little Egypt..." This landmark bluff and Native American site is located on State Route 147 in Pope County, Illinois and is part of the Shawnee National Forest. https://www.shawneeforest.com/millstone-bluff/ Accessed February 9, 2023.

"I remember when we moved to Flagstaff..." I refer to U2's video of their song, "I Still Haven't Found What I'm Looking For."

"I remember Flag's daily gladness…" A portion of this poem first appeared in different form in my poetry chapbook *Backyard Darwin*. Georgetown, KY: Finishing Line Press, 2019.

In his article "Darwin's Sacred Cause—The Unity of Humanity," Joshua M. Moritz argues that Darwin was deeply influenced by the evangelical-abolitionist belief in the unity of the human races—the "blood kinship"— ideas which influenced Darwin's *Origin of Species and The Descent of Man*. *Theology and Science*, 13(2015):1, http://doi.org/10.1018/14746700.2014.9879 91. Accessed August 2, 2022.

See also Sarah Kunezler, "Social Darwinism and the West as American Identity," British Association for Victorian Studies Postgraduate Pages, August 8, 2016. https://victorianist.wordpress.com/2016/08/08/social-darwinism-and-the-west-as-american-identity/. Accessed August 27, 2022.

"I remember when friend Carol …." I've reworked the Marguerite quotation for my own purpose: the original is from her *Heptameron,* Novel 38: "'Have you not heard,' said Geburon, 'that God always helps madmen, lovers, and drunkards?'" https://digital.library.upenn.edu/women/navarre/heptameron/heptameron.html#N38. Accessed October 25, 2022. The year before she died, Carol published an important book about Marguerite: Carol Thysell, *The Pleasure of Discernment: Marguerite de Navarre as Theologian*. Oxford: Oxford University Press, 2000.

"I remember eventful mornings…" The prevalent Eurocentric interpretation of the Canyon has been to perceive it as a grand and uninhabited wilderness, thus ignoring centuries of Native habitation, as well as Native perspectives on the Canyon. A helpful study is Sherri O'Neil, "Native American Perspectives in the Interpretation of Grand Canyon National Park." Prescott College ProQuest Dissertations Publishing, 2021. 28962701. https://www.proquest.com/openview/d440ba889ded910f2213ba9d13140e4f/1.pdf?pq-origsite=gscholar&cbl=18750&diss=y Accessed January 12, 2023.

"I remember our trips south to Prescott…" This section appeared in a slightly different form in my poetry book, *Galapagos Joy*. Georgetown, KY: Finishing Line Press, 2023. See Aaron Sachs, *The Humboldt Current: Nineteenth Century Exploration and the Roots of American Environmentalism*. New York: Penguin Books, 2006; Laura Dassow Walls, *Alexander von Humboldt and the Shaping of America*. Chicago: University of Chicago Press, 2009.

Prussian naturalist and polymath Alexander von Humboldt (1769-1859) inspired numerous naturalists, writers, and artists with his long research voyages and his comprehensive vision of the universe, *Cosmos*. His travel journals enchanted many, including Darwin. Humboldt's data-filled drawing of the Ecuadoran mountain Chimborazo, *"Naturgemälde,"* was very influential. Humboldt also published his *Political Essay on the Kingdom of New Spain* (1811). In time, to Humboldt's regret, his descriptions of Mexico precipitated U.S. interest in Mexican territories, and ultimately the Mexican War during the presidency of James K. Polk.

      Also: Alexander De Humboldt, *Political Essay on the Kingdom of New Spain*. Translated from the original French by John Black. Two volumes. New York: Printed and published by I. Riley, 1811. The book excited American readers already interested in the land west of the Mississippi. (See note above, "John Winthrop's preaching....") My copy was owned by "J. Stevens," perhaps John Harrington Stevens, who served with Winfield Scott's forces at the Battle of Vera Cruz in March 1847, which would explain the pencil sketch of the battle on the front free endpaper of Volume 2.

      The end quote is from Sidney E. Mead, *The Lively Experiment: The Shaping of Christianity in America* (New York: Harper & Row, 1963): "Bernard DeVoto... writing of the Indians in their last great preserve in the vast land 'across the wide Missouri'... says, 'the Indians might have been adapted to the nineteenth-century order and might have saved enough roots from their own order to grow in dignity and health in a changed world—if there had been time'. But once the fur trader and the farmer, the missionary and the schoolteacher, came, living out the inexorable myth of 'manifest destiny,' there was no time at all. For the Indian, no time to adapt—but even more tragically, for the white man no time for remorse, but only time for the labor in the cold and in the heat and in the vast places" (5)

"(On both sides of Civil War..." A fascinating book that examines both the injustices to Indians as well as the white perspective in the post-Civil War West is Peter Cozzens, *The Earth is Weeping: The Epic Story of the Indian Wars for the American West*. New York: Vintage Books, 2016.

"I remember in Arizona the beautiful cotton fields..." The Mill River runs near Whitney Ave. Eli Whitney, Sr. used the river for his machinery, and Eli, Jr. (the cotton gin inventor) used the river for his Armory, as well as to create New Haven's first public water supply. https://www.eliwhitney.org/museum/-historic-site/mill-river-and-waterfall Accessed February 15, 2023.

      On Silliman's visit with Humboldt, see Prof. Benjamin Silliman, *A Visit to Europe in 1851*. Volume II (New York: G. P. Putnam & Co., 1854) 318-322. On art that reflected the war and national mood, see Eleanor Jones Harvey, *The Civil War and American Art*. New Haven: Yale University Press, 2012. See also

Charles M. Segal and David C. Steinback, *Puritans, Indians & Manifest Destiny*. New York: G. P. Putnam's Sons, 1977.

Jelle Zeilinga de Boer and John Wareham discuss Thomas Cole's famous paintings, *The Course of Empire*, created in 1833-1836. In all the paintings, an asymmetrical mountain with a boulder at the peak appears in the background. The authors discuss the similarity, intentional or not, of the mountain's shape to that of West Rock. de Boer and Wareham, *New Haven's Sentinels* 128-132.

"Native artists know..." An earlier draft referred to feathers: the significant of feathers in Native American culture, in life and in art, see http://blog. nativepartnership.org/the-significance-of-feathers-in-native-cultures/ and also https://www.richardalois.com/symbolism/native-american-feather-meaning. Both accessed August 18, 2022.

The image of cave walls like skin is from a painting by Cherokee artist Bill Rabbit, "When My People Cried," discussed in the article about him in *Southwest Art*, 17(3), August 1987, 34-39. Sometimes it's good to keep old magazines around; I purchased this copy new when we first moved to Flagstaff, at the beloved McGaugh's Newsstand that operated downtown for 23 years.

"William Apess, a Pequot, knew...." The "poem" is a selection of words, mainly verbatim, from William Apess, "Eulogy for King Philip," 1836, https:// umvod.wordpress.com/apess-eulogy-speech-text/. Accessed August 2, 2022. I apologize for condensing this important work and I hope readers will seek out the whole speech online.

William Apess (1798-1839) was an ordained Methodist minister, part Pequot. He was perhaps the most significant activist for Native American rights during the antebellum era. He wrote about the Natives' loss of land to white settlers, even organizing a non-violent revolt of Mashpee Wampanoags in 1833. Among his written works are an autobiography, *A Son of the Forest*. Apess' 1836 lecture, *Eulogy on King Philip*, extolled Metacomet as a George Washington-type leader of his people.

On the importance and historical context of Apess, see Patricia Bizzell, "William Apess, Eulogy on King Philip (26 January 1836), *Voices of Democracy* 2 (2007): 79-98. https://voicesofdemocracy.umd.edu/wp-content/uploads/2010/07/bizzell-apess.pdf. Accessed August 2, 2022. See also the article (cited above) about Apess and Dr. Martin Luther King, Jr.

See also the chapter "Envisioning New England as Native Space: William Apess' *Eulogy on King Philip*," in Lisa Brooks, *The Common Pot: The Recovery of Native Space in the Northeast* (Minneapolis: University of Minnesota Press, 2008) 198-218.

I found an interesting article on aspects of Native American justice:

Laura Mirsky, "Restorative Justice Practices of Native American, First Nation and Other Indigenous People of North America: Part One", International Institute for Restorative Justice, April 27, 2004 https://www.iirp.edu/news/restorative-justice-practices-of-native-american-first-nation-and-other-indigenous-people-of-north-america-part-one. Accessed August 25, 2022.

A Native American acquaintance, who gave me very helpful comments, suggests reading "Chief Seattle's Speech" from 1854. https://suquamish.nsn.us/home/about-us/chief-seattle-speech/ Accessed March 25, 2023. On different versions of the speech, see https://cdn.centerforinquiry.org/wp-content/uploads/sites/29/1999/03/22164948/p44.pdf Accessed March 25, 2023.

V

"In time, my kin went West…." This poem is adapted from one first published in my book, *Four Mile*.

"(Grandma's grandpa Washburn…" My great-great-grandfather George Washburn, who is buried near Ramsey, IL, was a fourth cousin of Elihu Benjamin Washburne (1816-1887), a noted Illinois Republican congressman, ally of President Lincoln and President Grant, and the U.S. Minister to France in 1869-1877. Washburne also wrote an important biography of Illinois' second governor, Edward Coles, which I used for my first book, *High on the Okaw's Western Bank: Vandalia, Illinois, 1819-1839*. Urbana: University of Illinois Press, 1992. I am descended from George and his third wife Ellen, who also outlived her first two spouses.

"When I was a boy, 1960s …." This poem is adapted from one first published in my chapbook, *Little River*. Georgetown, KY: Finishing Line Press, 2017. It is also adapted from one in my poetry book, *Four Mile*. The present book connects to the *Four Mile* poem about my 3rd-great-grandparents David and Esther Washburn on p. 23.

I wrote this poem as I was beginning to think deeply about Native American heritage of my homelands. Working on the present project, I've learned how "Thoreau's desire to 'live deliberately' is part of a long American history of… 'playing Indian.' Nathaniel Hawthorne recognized this… describing how Thoreau was 'inclined to live a sort of Indian life among civilized men,' casting 'Indian' as an idealized metaphor for a more authentic experience of life… Thoreau lays claim not just to the land itself but to ideas about the land that have driven white American thought and politics for generations." Sarah

Blackwood, "Emerson and Thoreau's Fanatical Freedom." *The New Republic*, January 6, 2022. https://newrepublic.com/article/164828/emerson-thoreau-fanatical-freedom-transcendentalists. Accessed December 21, 2022.

"I walked Grandma's acres…" This poem is adapted from one in my book Four Mile.

"But this land is Native home…" This poem is adapted from one in my chapbook *Dreaming at the Electric Hobo,* Georgetown, KY: Finishing Line Press, 2017.

The story of the Native American man who visited ancestral places is from *History of Fayette County, Illinois* (Philadelphia: Brink, McDonough & Co., 1878), 10. Although he is partly writing out of regret for the loss of historical records about Native Americans, it is interesting that the author (in 1878) comments, "The result of white supremacy has been terrible to the red man. That is might have been otherwise will be apparent to any thoughtful person giving the subject consideration. Conquest by extermination seemed to be the policy of the psalm-singing Puritans, and has continued to be that of the Government nearly ever since" (9).

The story of the Gateway Arch includes many perspectives: see, for instance, http://npshistory.com/publications/jeff/index.htm Accessed February 9, 2023.

"In those young days…." This poem is adapted from one in my book *Four Mile.*

"In a div school spring…." The class was an Old Testament class taught by B. Davie Napier, a wonderful and distinguished professor at Yale and Stanford who, with his wife Joy, was an anti-war activist. The scripture references are Deuteronomy 16:20, Jeremiah 22:16, Amos 5:24, Isaiah 19:22-25, Matthew 6:33, Micah 6:8

Rabbi Craig Lewis, "Equity in Education: Let Every Student Shine," in Rabbi Barry H. Block, ed., *The Social Justice Torah Commentary* (New York: CCAR Press, 2021) 135-138. Rabbi Lewis has the image of Aaron's breastplate (Ex. 39:8-13) and the different qualities of each jewel. He makes a lovely analogy, which I've adapted here, of the preciousness and different needs of each human being. I learned of this wonderful, now-favorite book because of one of the contributors: friend and inspiration Maharat Rori Picker Neiss.

"The journey is a place of the Spirit…" *The plentitude of water…* is Revelation 22:1-2. I've paraphrased the Joshua story from the Bible verses Joshua 5:13-14, echoing the earlier story of Judge Goffe.

"Beauty of the Metacomet Ridge..." The words "bold precipice of columnar basalt, crowned with trap" are a combination of <u>two</u> quotations: Sir Charles Lyell, *Travels in North America, Canada, and Nova Scotia, with Geological Observations* (London: John Murray, 1845) 10, and also Sir Charles Lyell, *A Second Visit to the United States of North America* (London: John Murray, 1849) 235.

"*Learn justice...*" These final words are from William Apess' "Eulogy to King Philip", quoted and cited above.

Paul Stroble teaches philosophy and religious studies at Webster University in St. Louis and is retired adjunct faculty at Eden Theological Seminary. Previously he taught at the University of Akron, Indiana University Southeast, Louisville Seminary, and Northern Arizona University. He is a native of Vandalia (Fayette County), Illinois. A grantee of the National Endowment for the Humanities and the Louisville Institute, he has written several books, primarily church related, and numerous articles, essays, and curricular materials. He blogs at paulstroble.blogspot.com. His previous chapbooks with Finishing Line Press are *Dreaming at the Electric Hobo* (2015), *Little River* (2017), *Small Corner of the Stars* (2017), *Backyard Darwin* (2019), and *Galápagos Joy* (2023), as well as the full-length *Walking Lorton Bluff* (2020) and *Four Mile* (2022).